PETERHEAD PARISH

1801

CENSUS MATERIAL

As Compiled July 1801
by
Rev. George Moir

with Index
by
Aberdeen & N.E. Scotland
Family History Society

ISBN 0-947659-13-7

First published October 1993

by
Aberdeen & N.E Scotland
Family History Society

printed by:-
RAINBOW ENTERPRISES, Unit 2 Saxbone Development Centre, Dyce, ABERDEEN

CONTENTS

INTRODUCTION

Census records prior to 1841 listing people by name are rare, and to find one from as far back as 1801 is almost unique.

For a full description of census records and pre-1841 material, and advice on their use, recommended reading is:
"CENSUS RECORDS for SCOTTISH FAMILIES
AT HOME AND ABROAD"
by Gordon Johnson available from the FAMILY HISTORY SHOP,
164 King Street, Aberdeen

The Peterhead 1801 census record is in the form of a notebook collating the answers for the census questions. The census only required statistics, but listing the principal tenant by name helped in keeping track of the statistical data. There are many helpful comments on matters such as the state of the Church registers. The final statement of population is certified by Rev. George Moir, Minister of Peterhead, but this itself does not prove that he compiled all the data.

Enumerators in Scotland in 1801 were normally the local schoolmasters, but often the minister was also a schoolmaster, so George Moir may in fact have done all the census work.

As the notebook was his private record, and not part of his official returns, it remained with him and was eventually deposited in the local Peterhead Library, and after local government reorganisation in 1975 was transferred to the Local History Department of North-East Scotland Library Service, Meldrum Mcg Way, The Meadows Industrial Estate, Oldmeldrum, Aberdeenshire.

The Society was made aware of the existence of the document, and asked permission to index the contents and subsequently publish this book. N.E.S.L.S. gave their agreement to the publication, and provided photocopies for indexing purposes.

ACKNOWLEDGEMENTS

The Aberdeen and N.E. Scotland Family History Society wishes to thank N.E. Scotland Library Service for their encouraging approach to the publication of this document and for permission to reproduce the post card 'Town House and Broad Street, Peterhead' as used on the front cover.
Thanks are also due to those local members involved with the indexing and final preparation of the publication and for the accompanying maps.

PETERHEAD, JULY, 1801

Material for Answers to the
Questions contained in the schedule to an
Act entitled, an Act for taking an account of the
Population of Great Britain, and of the Increase
or Diminution therof; for the Parish of Peterhead,
in the County of Aberdeen, District of Buchan,
and Subdivision of Deer.

N.B. The First Question relates to Houses: and the First
Column of each page of this book contains the name of Streets in the
Town of Peterhead, or of the Estates etc. in the Country part of the
Parish: the second Column contains the Number of Inhabited Houses:
the Third the names of the Principal Tenants: the Fourth the number
of Families, in the several Houses: and the Fifth the Number of
Uninhabited Houses.

The Second Question relates to Persons: and the
the Sixth Column of each Page contains the Number of Males in the
several Houses: the Seventh the Number of Females; and the Eighth
the Sums of both.

The Third Question relates to Occupations
and the Ninth Column of each Page contains the Number of Persons in
the several Houses chiefly employed in Agriculture; the Tenth the
Number of Persons chiefly employed in Trade, Manufacture, or Handicraft;
The Eleventh the Number of all other Persons not belonging to the two
preceding Classes; and the Twelfth the Sums of all the three, corresponding
with the Sums of Males and Females in the Eighth Column.

Address	No. House	Name of Principal Tenant			Col 4	Col 5	Col 6	Col 7	Col 8	Col 9	Col 10	Col 11	Col 12
Quinzie	1	BURNETT	Alexander		2		2	5	7		2	5	7
"	2	KING	James		1		2	1	3		2	1	3
"	3	CLACKIE	George		1		2	2	4		2	2	4
"	4	SMITH	John		3		7	10	17		2	15	17
"	5	ANNAND		Widow	1	1		3	3		1	2	3
"	6	LAMB		Mrs	3		6	4	10		1	9	10
"	7	SCOTT	William		1		2	2	4		2	2	4
"	8	ANDERSON	John		1		1	1	2			2	2
"	9	HENDERSON	Robert		1		2	2	4		2	2	4
"	10	DANIEL	Andrew		1		1	3	4		2	2	4
"	11	THOM	John		1		4	2	6		3	3	6
"	12	HUTCHISON	John	Mr	1		5	8	13		1	12	13
"	13	ROBERTSON	Thomas		1		5	6	11		5	6	11
"	14	HUTCHISON		Capt'n	1	1	3	1	4			4	4
"	15	MILNE	George		3		3	7	10		1	9	10
Broadgate	16	BENNET	John		1		3	2	5		3	2	5
"	17	OGSTON	Robert		1		7	4	11		3	8	11
"	18	SMITH	Andrew		1		2	2	4		1	3	4
"	19	CRAWFORD	Charles		4		9	15	24		7	17	24
"	20	LOW	Mary		1			1	1			1	1
"	21	MORRICE	John		3		4	5	9		1	8	9
"	22	ROBERTSON	Andrew		2		2	2	4		1	3	4
"	23	ARBUTHNOT	James	Mr	1		4	2	6		2	4	6
					36	2	76	90	166		44	122	166

Address	No. House	Name of Principal Tenant			Col 4	Col 5	Col 6	Col 7	Col 8	Col 9	Col 10	Col 11	Col 12
Broadgate	24	HUNTER		Mrs	3			3	3			3	3
"	25	BARCLAY	William	Mrs	2		1	9	10		4	6	10
"	26	ABEL			2		3	3	6		3	3	6
"	27	SHAND		Mr	1		1	2	3			3	3
"	28	KILGOUR		Mrs	1			2	2			2	2
"	29	ABERNETHY	William		2		2	3	5		2	3	5
"	30	ROBERTSON		Mrs	2			3	3			3	3
"	31	SMITH		Mrs	1			3	3			3	3
"	32	BRODIE		Mrs	4		2	8	10			10	10
"	33	BREBNER	William		2		4	4	8		1	7	8
"	34	STEPHEN	John		2		3	4	7		3	4	7
"	35	KAY		Mrs	2		1	2	3			3	3
"	36	WILSON		Mrs	2		1	2	3		1	2	3
"	37	LIVINGSTONE		Mrs	1			3	3			3	3
"	38	BOGGIE	John		2		4	3	7		4	3	7
"	39	REID	John		3	1	3	3	6		1	5	6
"	40	DUNCAN	John		1		2	1	3		1	2	3
"	41	ARBUTHNOT	Thomas	Mr	1		6	7	13		1	12	13
"	42	SOUTTER	John		1		1	4	5			5	5
"	43	CHEYNE		Mrs	2		3	4	7		1	6	7
"	44	WEBSTER		Widow	3			4	4			4	4
"	45	FORBES	James	Junior	1		3	4	7		3	4	7
"	46	MILNE	John		1		1	3	4		2	2	4
"	47	PETRIE		Miss	2			5	5			5	5
					44	1	41	89	130		27	103	130
					80	3	117	179	296		71	225	296

Address	No. House	Name of Principal Tenant		Col 4	Col 5	Col 6	Col 7	Col 8	Col 9	Col 10	Col 11	Col 12
Broadgate	48	TRAIL	Jean	1			1	1			1	1
"	49	MACLEAN	Mrs	1		3	5	8			8	8
"	50	WILSON	Andrew	2		4	2	6		2	4	6
"	51	MILNE	Isabel	1			1	1			1	1
"	52	MAVOR	George	1		1	1	2		1	1	2
"	53	ARTHUR	Andrew	2		3	2	5		2	3	5
"	54	GIBB	Robert	2		7	3	10		5	5	10
"	55	SAUNDERS	John	2		5	5	10		5	6	10
"	56	COGLAN	John	2		1	11	12		4	12	12
"	57	MUTCH	John	1		2	3	5			5	5
"	58	SMITH	Thomas	2		5	5	10		2	8	10
"	59	CUMINE	Charles	1		3	3	6		1	5	6
"	60	MORISON	Joseph	2		6	1	7			7	7
"	61	DAVIDSON	John	1		3	2	5		1	4	5
"	62	WILSON	Theodore	1		4	3	7			7	7
"	63	ADAMSON	William	4		6	12	18		2	16	18
"	64	DAVIDSON	Andrew	2		2	1	3			3	3
"	65	FORREST	Thomas	2		4	2	6		1	5	6
"	66	WILLIAMSON	James	3		1	4	5			5	5
"	67	SCOTT	Thomas	1		1	1	2			2	2
"	68	CRAIGHEAD	James	2		1	2	3		1	2	3
"	69	WATSON	James	6		13	16	29		4	25	29
"	70	HUTCHISON	James	1		3	2	5		1	4	5
"	71	HUTCHISON	James	3		10	7	17		1	16	17
"	72	THOMSON	Mrs	1			2	2		1	1	2
"	73	KEITH	George	2		2	2	4		3	1	4
"	74	DAVIDSON	Thomas	2		6	2	8		4	4	8
				51	3	96	101	197		36	161	197
				131		213	280	493		107	386	493

Address	No. House	Name of Principal Tenant		Col 4	Col 5	Col 6	Col 7	Col 8	Col 9	Col 10	Col 11	Col 12
Broadgate	75	NEDDRIE	Charles	1		2	2	4		2	2	4
"	76	TAIT	Alexander	3		4	3	7		2	5	7
"	77	LIBERTY	Mrs	1			2	2			2	2
"	78	FINDLAY	Mrs	3		2	5	7		1	6	7
"	79	FRASER	James	4		1	8	9		1	7	9
"	80	OGSTON	George	2		3	2	5	1		5	5
"	81	KEIR	Robert	6		10	10	20		7	13	20
"	82	MILNE	Isabel	1			1	1			1	1
"	83	SHEWAN	Robert	1		1	2	3		1	2	3
"	84	DAVIDSON	William	1		3	2	5			5	5
"	85	FORBES	Andrew	1		1	2	3		1	2	3
"	86	BURNETT	Mrs	1		1	1	2			2	2
"	87	DUNCAN	James	2		2	1	3		2	1	3
"	88	FORSYTH	John	1		2	2	4		1	3	4
"	89	MUTCH	Katharine	1			3	3		1	2	3
"	90	ANDERSON	James	1		2	4	6		1	5	6
"	91	ROBERTSON	Mrs	4		1	4	5			5	5
"	92	LYON	George	4		9	10	19		3	16	19
"	93	WEBSTER	James	2		5	3	8		1	7	8
"	94	SMITH	James	2		3	5	8		1	7	8
"	95	MUTCH	Barbara	1			2	2		1	1	2
"	96	MILNE	Mr	1		2	3	5			5	5
"	97	MITCHEL	Robert	2		5	6	11		3	8	11
"	98	MATTHEW	Thomas	2		8	4	12		8	4	12
"	99	CONNAN	Alexander	1		3	3	6		2	4	6
"	100	BUCHAN	Mrs	1			3	3			3	3
"	101	LAING	Dr	1		2	7	9			9	9
				51	3	72	100	172	1	39	132	172
				182		285	380	665		146	518	665

Address	No. House	Name of Principal Tenant		Col 4	Col 5	Col 6	Col 7	Col 8	Col 9	Col 10	Col 11	Col 12
Broadgate	102	FORBES	James	1		3	7	10		2	8	10
"	103	ARGO	James	1		1		1		1		1
"	104	FRASER	Mrs	1			2	2			2	2
"	105	SHIVES	Alexander	1		1	1	2		1	1	2
"	106	SHIVES	John	1		2	1	3		2	1	3
"	107	SHIVES	William	1		4	7	11		1	10	11
"	108	SCOTT (junior)	Mr	1		6	4	10		1	9	10
"	109	CORDINER	Mrs	1		1	3	4		1	3	4
"	110	DALLACHY	John	3		6	7	13		4	9	13
"	111	YULE	Alexander	2		3	2	5		1	4	5
"	112	LEASK	William	2		6	5	11		4	7	11
"	113	QUIRIE	Alexander	2		2	4	6		1	5	6
"	114	HECTOR	Elspet	1			1	1			1	1
"	115	BURD	Mrs	3		3	4	7		2	5	7
"	116	DALGARNO	Mrs	1			2	2			2	2
"	117	HENDERSON	Patrick	3		2	5	7		1	6	7
"	118	OGILVIE	Alexander	2		2	3	5		2	3	5
"	119	DUNCAN	Charles	1		3	1	4		3	1	4
"	120	JAFFRAY	James	1		1	3	4		1	3	4
"	121	MESS	Christian	1			1	1			1	1
"	122	LYON	Andrew	2		4	4	8		1	7	8
"	123	GARDEN	John	1		1	2	3		1	2	3
"	124	SMITH	Mrs	1			1	1			1	1
"	125	DUNCAN	Margaret	1			1	1			1	1
"	126	CHRISTIE	Alexander	2		3	2	5		2	3	5
"	127	CLOCKIE	George	2		4	1	5		4	1	5
				39	3	58	74	132	1	36	96	132
				221		343	454	797		182	614	797

Address	No. House	Name of Principal Tenant			Col 4	Col 5	Col 6	Col 7	Col 8	Col 9	Col 10	Col 11	Col 12
Broadgate	128	IMLAY	James		1		1	1	2		1	1	2
" "	129	ALEXANDER	Gilbert		1		6	4	10		1	9	10
" "	130	MACINTOSH		Capt'n	1		7	4	11		1	10	11
" "	131	ELLES		Capt'n	1		2	7	9		2	7	9
" "	132	SMITH	George		2		4	8	12		2	10	12
" "	133	CHALMERS	Robert		1		1	3	4		1	3	4
" "	134	GIBSON	William		1		2	1	3		2	1	3
" "	135	WEBSTER	John		1		3	5	8		2	6	8
" "	136	CATTO	Charles		1		1	2	3		1	2	3
" "	137	GORDON	James		1		3	2	5		1	4	5
" "	138	MACKIE	Alexander		2		2	1	3		1	2	3
North Shore	139	BRODIE	William		1		1	4	5			5	5
" "	140	HIRD	John		1		1	2	3		1	2	3
" "	141	STEWART		Mrs	2		4	4	8		2	6	8
" "	142	FORREST	Peter		1		2	6	8			8	8
" "	143	JACK	Thomas		2		6	4	10		2	8	10
" "	144	SMITH	Thomas		1		2	1	3		2	1	3
" "	145	WHITE	Alexander		1		1	1	2			2	2
" "	146	BISSET	Janet		3		2	5	7			7	7
" "	147	TAYLOR	John		6		8	9	17		2	15	17
" "	148	MATTHEW	James		1		2	2	4		1	3	4
" "	149	GRAY	George		1		5	2	7			7	7
" "	150	CLARK	David		2		4	3	7		2	5	7
" "	151	CLARK	Alexander		2		2	2	4			4	4
" "	152	ROSS	Donald		3		3	6	9			9	9
" "	153	SANGSTER	James		2		3	3	6		1	5	6
					42	3	78	92	170	1	28	142	170
					263		421	546	967		210	756	967

Address	No. House	Name of Principal Tenant		Col 4	Col 5	Col 6	Col 7	Col 8	Col 9	Col 10	Col 11	Col 12
North Shore	154	PHILIP	Alexander	2		2	3	5		2	3	5
" "	155	BRODIE	James	3		6	5	11		2	9	11
" "	156	CORMACK	George	6		7	6	13		3	10	13
" "	157	BINNIE	Robert	2		3	3	6			6	6
" "	158	BUCHAN	John	2		3	5	8	1		7	8
" "	159	MAIN	Robert	3		7	3	10		3	7	10
" "	160	TAIT	Jean	1			1	1			1	1
" "	161	YEATS	Alexander	1		2	1	3		1	2	3
" "	162	SCOTT	William	4		4	7	11		1	10	11
" "	163	SOUTTER	John	1			3	3			3	3
Longate	164	MACDONALD	William	2		4	4	8		2	6	8
" "	165	CHEYNE	John	1		2	3	5		1	4	5
" "	166	GORDON	John	2		3	2	5			5	5
" "	167	PIRIE	Jean	4			4	4			4	4
" "	168	MOIR		1			1	1			1	1
" "	169	BUCHAN	Peter	4		5	9	14		1	13	14
" "	170	DAVIDSON		3		5	5	10		1	9	10
" "	171	MATTHEW	George	1		1	1	2		1	1	2
" "	172	STRACHAN	William	1		1	5	6		1	5	6
" "	173	HAY	Robert	2		2	1	3		1	2	3
" "	174	RANTON	Thomas	1		2	4	6		1	5	6
" "	175	THOMSON	James	1		4	2	6			6	6
" "	176	ROBERTSON	William	1		3	1	4	1		3	4
" "	177	LAWSON	William	2		4	4	8			8	8
" "	178	REID		4		1	12	13		1	12	13
" "	179	MUTCH	George	4		6	8	14		3	11	14
				59	3	77	103	180	2	25	153	180
						498	649	1147	3	235	909	1147
				322				1147				1147

Address	No. House	Name of Principal Tenant			Col 4	Col 5	Col 6	Col 7	Col 8	Col 9	Col 10	Col 11	Col 12
Longate	180	ROBERTSON	Thomas		3		5	3	8		1	7	8
"	181	BRANDS	Andrew		3		3	4	7		3	4	7
"	182	GORDON	Alexander		1		4	5	9		1	8	9
"	183	SIM	George		1		4	4	8			8	8
"	184	TODD		Mrs	5		5	8	13		2	11	13
"	185	MOIR	John		1		1	3	4			4	4
"	186	SELLER	William		1		1	3	4		1	3	4
"	187	RITCHIE	James		1		1	2	3			3	3
"	188	CHISHOLM	John		1		3	5	8		1	7	8
"	189	RITCHIE	Mary		1		1	5	6		1	5	6
"	190	DAWSON		Mrs	1			2	2			2	2
"	191	MORICE	James		1			4	4			4	4
"	192	SINCLAIR	Helen		1			3	3			3	3
"	193	MACKIE		Mrs	1		2	2	4		2	2	4
"	194	ROBERTSON	William		1		6	3	9		2	7	9
"	195	LIND		Mrs	2		1	4	5			5	5
"	196	MITCHEL	Charles		1		5	3	8		2	6	8
"	197	FINDLATER	William		3		7	9	16		1	15	16
"	198	MACKENZIE	Isabel		1			1	1			1	1
"	199	GERRIE	John		2		5	3	8		2	6	8
"	200	ROBB	Elspet		2			2	2			2	2
"	201	TAYLOR		Mrs	2			2	2			2	2
"	202	MACKIE	Alexander		2		2	4	6		3	3	6
"	203	WILLOX	George		2		4	3	7		2	5	7
"	204	RHIND	William		1		4	3	7		4	3	7
"	205	ROBERTSON	James		1		1	5	6		1	5	6
					42	3	65	95	160	3	29	131	160
					364	3	563	744	1307	3	264	1040	1307

Address	No. House	Name of Principal Tenant			Col 4	Col 5	Col 6	Col 7	Col 8	Col 9	Col 10	Col 11	Col 12
Longate	206	SCOTT		Mr	1		1	1	2			2	2
"	207	ADAMS	Robert		1		2	1	3		1	2	3
"	208	KIER	Mary		1			1	1			1	1
"	209	GORDON		Mrs	1			3	3			3	3
"	210	SELLER	John		1		3	4	7		1	6	7
"	211	ROBERTSON	Alexander		1		2	2	4		2	2	4
"	212	ROBERTSON	John		1		2	5	7		1	6	7
"	213	GREIG	Alexander		4		11	7	18		3	15	18
"	214	GRAY	Elisabeth		1			1	1			1	1
"	215	WILL	William		2		7	7	14		2	12	14
"	216	RAY	John		2		2	5	7		1	6	7
"	217	FORBES	James		1		1	2	3		1	2	3
"	218	HUTCHISON		Mrs	1		2	2	4			4	4
"	219	GREGORY	John		2		6	3	9		1	8	9
"	220	SMITH	William		1		4	5	9		1	8	9
"	221	HACKET	William		1		1	3	4		1	3	4
"	222	MACLALLEAN	John		1		4	2	6		2	4	6
"	223	WARDEN	John		1		3	4	7			7	7
"	224	SLICER	George		1		1	1	2		1	1	2
"	225	BIRNIE	Alexander		3		6	5	11		5	6	11
"	226	RIACH	John		4		1	4	5			5	5
"	227	HUTCHISON	John		3		1	7	8			8	8
"	228	MITCHEL	James		1		3	1	4		1	3	4
"	229	DINNIES	John		3		5	8	13		2	11	13
"	230	CLARK	James		1		4	4	8		3	5	8
"	231	TRAIL	James		3		6	9	15		1	14	15
"	232	SCOTT	Alexander		1		3	1	4			4	4
					44	3	81	98	179	3	30	149	179
					408		644	842	1486		294	1189	1486

Address	No. House	Name of Principal Tenant		Col 4	Col 5	Col 6	Col 7	Col 8	Col 9	Col 10	Col 11	Col 12
Longate	233	WILLIAMSON	Robert	4		3	4	7		1	6	7
"	234	STRATH	John	3		2	3	5		1	4	5
"	235	PHILIP	John	3		5	4	9		2	7	9
"	236	FERGUSON	George	1		1	1	2		1	1	2
"	237	HAY	Thomas	3		4	6	10			10	10
"	238	HUTCHISON	Janet	4		1	7	8			8	8
"	239	THOM	John	2		1	3	4		1	3	4
"	240	WATT	Thomas	4		5	5	10		1	9	10
Ronheads	241	LOW	James	1		2	2	4			4	4
"	242	KNOX	Andrew	1		2	2	4			4	4
"	243	WILL	Elisabeth	2			2	2			2	2
"	244	BROOK	Peter	1		2	1	3			3	3
"	245	BROOK	Mrs	1			2	2			2	2
"	246	BAIN	Robert	1		1	1	2			1	2
"	247	FORREST	Alexander	1		1	2	3	1		2	3
"	248	BROOK	Mary	2		3	2	5		1	5	5
"	249	SKINNER	Margaret	1			1	1			1	1
"	250	SANGSTER	John	2		1	3	4			4	4
"	251	MURISON	Marjory	2		1	2	3			3	3
"	252	GRAY	John	3		5	3	8		4	4	8
"	253	FYFE	Charles	1		1	4	5		1	4	5
"	254	MURRAY	Hugh	1		1	4	5			5	5
"	255	DAVIDSON	John	1		2	3	5			5	5
"	256	THOM	James	1		2	1	3			3	3
"	257	BRUCE	William	1		4	3	7			7	7
"	258	CHEYNE	James	1		1	1	2			2	2
"	259	LORIMER	George	2		2	1	3		1	2	3
				50	3	53	73	126	1	14	111	126
				458		697	915	1612	4	308	1300	1612

Address	No. House	Name of Principal Tenant		Col 4	Col 5	Col 6	Col 7	Col 8	Col 9	Col 10	Col 11	Col 12
Ronheads	260	LILLIE	William	1		1	3	4	1		3	4
"	261	WEBSTER	James	1		2	2	4		2	2	4
"	262	SLAKER	James	1		2	1	3			3	3
"	263	WATT	Christian	1			3	3			3	3
"	264	SMITH	Charles	1		2	2	4			4	4
"	265	WATSON	Janet	1			1	1			1	1
"	266	DAVIDSON	Alexander	1		1	1	2			2	2
"	267	DAVIDSON	Christian	1			1	1			1	1
"	268	STEVENSON	William	1		1	1	2			2	2
"	269	CLARK	Alexander	2		2	2	4			4	4
"	270	BISSET	Elisabeth	1			1	1			1	1
"	271	GRAY	Isabel	2		2	2	4			4	4
"	272	MUTCHISON	George	1		3	1	4			4	4
"	273	WILSON	John	1		4	4	8		1	7	8
"	274	MACGILLAVRAY	Robert	1		4	4	8		1	7	8
"	275	BAXTER	Margaret	2		2	5	7			7	7
"	276	MACKENZIE	Calib	1		2	2	4			4	4
"	277	WEBSTER	James	1		3	1	4			4	4
"	278	GRAY	Janet	2			2	2			2	2
"	279	BUTTER	James	3		2	4	6			6	6
"	280	CROOKSHANK	John	1		1	2	3			3	3
"	281	THOM	William	1		2	2	4			4	4
"	282	DUNBAR	Peter	1		1	2	3		1	2	3
"	283	SMITH	William	2		1	2	3			3	3
"	284	HUTCHISON	George	1		2	3	5		3	2	5
"	285	ROBERTSON	William	1		1	5	6		3	3	6
"	286	BUCHAN	Robert	1		1	2	3		1	2	3
"	287	SOUTTER	Mrs	1		1	2	3			3	3
"	288	SOUTTER	Janet	1		1	3	4			4	4
"	289	ROBB	Elspet	1			2	2			2	2
				37	3	44	68	112	1	12	99	112
				495		741	983	1724	5	320	1399	1724

Address	No. House	Name of Principal Tenant		Col 4	Col 5	Col 6	Col 7	Col 8	Col 9	Col 10	Col 11	Col 12
Ronheads	290	MACKIE	William	1		2	1	3		2	1	3
"	291	LEASK	James	1		4	2	6		4	2	6
"	292	SOUTTER	Mrs	1			1	1			1	1
"	293	SOUTTER	Gilbert	1		1	1	2		2		2
"	294	SOUTTER	Alexander	1		5	5	10		5	5	10
"	295	TAYLOR	Christian	1			2	2			2	2
"	296	DAVIDSON	Mrs	1		2	3	5			5	5
"	297	CORDINER	James	1		3	5	8		5	3	8
"	298	MACKIE	John	1			1	1			1	1
"	299	ROBERTSON	James	1		3	3	6		5	1	6
"	300	STRACHAN	Alexander	1		2	2	4		2	2	4
"	301	CORDINER	Elspet	1			1	1			1	1
"	302	MILNE	Christian	1			2	2			2	2
"	303	MURDOCH	John	1		1	2	3			3	3
"	304	GERRIE	Robert	1		2	2	4		3	1	4
"	305	DUN	Janet	1			1	1			1	1
"	306	DUNCAN	Alexander	1		1	2	3		2	1	3
"	307	DUNCAN	Widow	1		2	2	4		3	1	4
"	308	DINNET	John	1		1	2	3		3		3
"	309	DUN	Elisabeth	1		1	1	2		1	1	2
"	310	ROBERTSON	Alexander	1		3	5	8		5	3	8
"	311	GERRIE	Alexander	1		1	6	7			7	7
"	312	SANGSTER	Robert	1		1	4	5			5	5
"	313	BRUCE	Anne	1			2	2			2	2
"	314	KEITH	Alexander	1		4	4	8		4	4	8
"	315	BUCHAN	John	1		1	2	3		3		3
"	316	ROBB	Peter	1		2	3	5		4	1	5
"	317	CORMACK	Widow	1			2	2			2	2
"	318	DUN	Robert	1		5	4	9		6	3	9
"	319	BUCHAN	George	1		3	3	6		5	1	6
				30	3	50	76	126	5	64	62	126
				525		791	1059	1850		384	1461	1850

Address	No. House	Name of Principal Tenant		Col 4	Col 5	Col 6	Col 7	Col 8	Col 9	Col 10	Col 11	Col 12
Ronheads	320	SOUTTER	Mary	1			2	2			2	2
"	321	MILNE	George	1			5	5			5	5
"	322	TAYLOR	William	1		3	3	6		3	3	6
"	323	TAYLOR	William	1		1		1			1	1
"	324	GRAY	James	1		2	3	5		1	4	5
"	325	SANGSTER	Widow	1			1	1		1		1
"	326	BINNIE	Alexander	1		2	2	4		2	2	4
"	327	ROBB	George	1		1	3	4		4		4
"	328	SEMPLE	John	1		1	3	4		1	3	4
"	329	ROBB	Jean	1			1	1		1		1
"	330	THOMSON	William	1		1	2	3			3	3
"	331	TURRIFF	David	1		2	1	3			3	3
"	332	ROBERTSON	Alexander	2		4	4	8		2	6	8
"	333	SOUTTER	William	2		3	2	5		1	4	5
"	334	CORMACK	William	1		5	1	6		1	5	6
"	335	CORMACK	Janet	1			1	1			1	1
"	336	ALEXANDER	Isabel	1			1	1			1	1
"	337	MORISON	George	2		2	2	4			4	4
"	338	JACK	Lewis	3		1	4	5			5	5
Backgate	339	GALL	Alexander	2		3	4	7		1	6	7
"	340	CHEYNE	William	1		1	4	5		1	4	5
"	341	DUNCAN	Mrs	1			1	1			1	1
"	342	BRUCE	William	2		2	2	4		1	3	4
"	343	MINTO	Widow	4		5	8	13			13	13
"	344	ROBB	Andrew	1		1	1	2		1	1	2
"	345	MILNE	James	1		2	4	6		2	4	6
"	346	STUART	James	1		3	2	5		1	4	5
"	347	KEITH	Mrs	2		1	4	5			5	5
"	348	LAWRENCE	George	2		3	5	8			8	8
"	349	WALLACE	Janet	4		5	7	12			12	12
"	350	CAIRD	Anne	4			7	7			7	7
				49	3	54	90	144	5	24	120	144
				574		845	1149	1994		408	1581	1994

Address	No. House	Name of Principal Tenant			Col 4	Col 5	Col 6	Col 7	Col 8	Col 9	Col 10	Col 11	Col 12
Backgate	351	FORBES	Thomas		3		3	4	7			7	7
"	352	FRASER	Donald		1		1	4	5			5	5
"	353	MILNE	Margaret		2			2	2			2	2
"	354	BODDIE	Alexander		1		1	2	3			3	3
"	355	THOMSON	James		2		3	6	9		2	7	9
"	356	THOM	James		1		2	1	3		2	1	3
"	357	FARQUHAR	James		4		5	3	8		1	7	8
"	358	CRIGHTON	Alexander		2		2	1	3		1	2	3
"	359	REID		Mrs	3		2	3	5			5	5
"	360	CAMPBELL	Alex'r		1		3	3	6			6	6
"	361	WALLACE	William		1		1	5	6		1	5	6
"	362	WILL	Alexander		3		7	4	11		4	7	11
Cairdwell Road	363	BOWMAN	James		4		1	6	7		1	6	7
"	364	ROSS	James		2		3	4	7		3	4	7
"	365	REID	James		3		4	4	8		3	5	8
"	366	SLORACH	John		2		2	5	7		2	5	7
"	367	DUNBAR	Rob't		4		4	7	11		2	9	11
"	368	GRANT	Patrick		1		6	6	12		2	10	12
"	369	MURISON	George		4		4	12	16		1	15	16
"	370	MACPHERSON	John		5		10	4	14		5	9	14
"	371	CAMPBELL	James		4		7	4	11		2	9	11
"	372	ABERNETHY	Andrew		4		6	5	11		3	8	11
"	373	CROOKSHANK	William		4		5	9	14		3	11	14
"	374	FYFE	Charles		6		8	11	19		1	18	19
"	375	MILNE	William		3		3	5	8		1	7	8
"	376	MATTHEW	George		4		2	5	7			7	7
"	377	WEMYSS	Walter		1			2	2			2	2
St.Peters Lane	378	ALLAN	William		5		6	10	16		3	13	16
"	379	FORREST	William		4		2	9	11		4	7	11
"	380	WEBSTER	John		2		2	3	5		1	4	5
"	381	FORREST	James		2		2	5	7			7	7
					88	3	107	154	261		48	213	261
					662		952	1303	2255	5	456	1794	2255

Address	No. House	Name of Principal Tenant		Col 4	Col 5	Col 6	Col 7	Col 8	Col 9	Col 10	Col 11	Col 12
St. Peters Lane	382	BARCLAY	John	3		4	7	11		4	7	11
"	383	SIMPSON	Alexander	2		5	3	8		4	4	8
"	384	GALLOWAY	Mrs	2			7	7		1	6	7
"	385	HUTCHISON	George	2		2	2	4		2	2	4
"	386	DALRYMPLE	Robert	3		7	10	17		2	15	17
"	387	MAITLAND	Adam	3		3	7	10		2	8	10
"	388	MOWAT	Mrs	1		2	5	7			7	7
"	389	AULD	Mrs	1			1	1			1	1
"	390	REID	Alexander	2		2	4	6			6	6
"	391	CHEYNE	Thomas	1		1	1	2		1	1	2
"	392	BOYS	John	1		1	1	2		1	1	2
"	393	YOUNGSON	John	3		7	6	13		4	9	13
Shorehead	394	ARGO	James	2		8	4	12		2	10	12
"	395	MACDONALD	Kenneth	1		1	3	4		1	3	4
"	396	SKELTON	James	1		3	4	7		1	6	7
"	397	MITCHEL	William	2		4	7	11		2	9	11
"	398	CUMINE	Alexander	1		1	2	3		1	2	3
"	399	GARDEN	George	1		1	1	2			2	2
"	400	WOOD	George	2		2	3	5			5	5
"	401	CHRISTIE	Margaret	1			1	1			1	1
"	402	FERGUSON	Capt'n	2		4	5	9			9	9
"	403	PATERSON	John	1		2	2	4		2	2	4
"	404	HARVEY	Mr	1		1	1	2			2	2
"	405	SHARP	Mrs	3		1	5	6		1	5	6
"	406	MACKENZIE	John	1		1		1			1	1
"	407	HURRIE	Gilbert	5		3	10	13			13	13
"	408	FRASER	Mrs	1		1	4	5			5	5
"	409	DAVIDSON	William	2		3	5	8		1	7	8
"	410	ARBUTHNOT	Misses	2			4	4			4	4
"	411	DARG	Andrew	1		3	1	4		3	1	4
				54	3	73	116	189	5	35	154	189
				716	3	1025	1419	2444	5	491	1948	2444

Address	No. House	Name of Principal Tenant			Col 4	Col 5	Col 6	Col 7	Col 8	Col 9	Col 10	Col 11	Col 12
Well-Street	412	WALLACE		John	1		9	6	15			15	15
"	413	PARKS	Misses		1			5	5		5		5
"	414	ROBERTSON	Baillie		1		3	2	5			5	5
"	415	SKELTON		George	1		2	3	5		1	4	5
"	416	ABERDEEN	Lord		1			1	1			1	1
"	417	ANDERSON	Dr.		1		3	3	6		2	4	6
"	418	FORBES	Mrs		1			3	3			3	3
"	419	ANDERSON		James	2		2	7	9		1	8	9
"	420	ARBUTHNOT	Mr		2		4	3	7		4	3	7
"	421	BROWN		Charles	1		1	3	4		1	3	4
"	422	JACK		William	1		1	1	2		1	1	2
"	423	ROBB		Andrew	1		3	2	5		3	2	5
"	424	MATTHEW	Mrs		1			2	2			2	2
"	425	LESLIE		John	1		4	4	8		4	4	8
"	426	STEWART		Patrick	2		5	1	6		4	2	6
"	427	CROOKSHANK		John	1		1	3	4			4	4
James' St.	428	PARKS	Misses		1			4	4		4		4
"	429	ARBUTHNOT	Mrs		2		2	3	5		1	4	5
"	430	FORBES	Mr		1		1	3	4			4	4
"	431	SIMS	Mr		1		4	5	9			9	9
"	432	MATTHEW		Alexander	3		8	5	13		3	10	13
"	433	JAFFRAY		John	3	1	6	4	10		2	8	10
"	434	FINDLATER		John	2		1	2	3			3	3
"	435	STUART		Thomas	1		2	4	6		1	5	6
"	436	ANDERSON		James	1		2	3	5			5	5
"	437	BRANDS		Alex'r	1		2	4	6			6	6
"	438	PATERSON		William	1		2	2	4		1	3	4
"	439	RAINIE		William	1		3	2	5		3	2	5
"	440	BLACK		Thomas	1		4	2	6		1	5	6
					38	1	75	92	167	5	42	125	167
					754	4	1100	1511	2611		533	2073	2611

Address	No. House	Name of Principal Tenant			Col 4	Col 5	Col 6	Col 7	Col 8	Col 9	Col 10	Col 11	Col 12
James' St.	441	MILNE	James		1		4	5	9		4	5	9
"	442	GRANT	John		1		2	2	4		2	2	4
"	443	BALFOUR	George		2		1	3	4		3	1	4
"	444	DAVIDSON	William		4		7	8	15		2	13	15
"	445	CLARK	John		4		3	9	12			12	12
"	446	SKINNER	Robert		1		1	2	3		1	2	3
Merchant St.	447	TAYLOR	William		1		4	3	7		4	3	7
"	448	FARQUHAR	William		1		1	2	3		3		3
"	449	FORBES	Alexander		2		3	9	12		2	10	12
"	450	ROBERTSON	William		2		3	2	5			5	5
"	451	WILL	John		1		1	1	2		1	1	2
"	452	JAFFRAY		Mrs	2		1	3	4			4	4
"	453	HAY	William		1		3	4	7		3	4	7
"	454	BODDIE		Mrs	2		1	3	4			4	4
"	455	JOHNSTON	James		2		3	3	6		3	3	6
"	456	HAY	Robert		2		3	3	6		2	4	6
"	457	ROBB	Alexander		2		3	2	5		3	2	5
"	458	GILLIE	John		1		1	4	5			5	5
"	459	SCANDRETT	James		2		4	4	8		2	6	8
"	460	LEITH	John		1		2	2	4			4	4
"	461	TAYLOR	Isabel		2		1	4	5			5	5
"	462	CRAIG	Alexander		1		1	1	2			2	2
"	463	BRIMS	John		2		2	2	4		1	3	4
"	464	THOMSON	Elisabeth		3		1	8	9			9	9
"	465	HOWIE	William		2		1	4	5			5	5
"	466	WOOD	John		1		2	1	3		2	1	3
"	467	TORRY		Mr	1		3	8	11			11	11
"	468	FORBES		Mrs	1			2	2			2	2
"	469	JAMIESON		Dr.	1		4	5	9		1	8	9
"	470	SOUTTER		Mrs	1		2	3	5		2	3	5
					50	4	68	112	180	5	41	139	180
					804		1168	1623	2791		574	2212	2791

Address	No. House	Name of Principal Tenant		Col 4	Col 5	Col 6	Col 7	Col 8	Col 9	Col 10	Col 11	Col 12
Merchant St.	471	HUTCHISON	Capt'n	1		7	7	14		4	10	14
"	472	BAILLIE		1	1			3			3	3
"	473	IRONSIDE John	Mrs	1		2	3	4		1	3	4
"	474	BENNET James		2		3	2	5		2	3	5
Back of	475	BRUCE Robert		2		2	1	3		2	1	3
Town-House	476	MITCHEL John		1		1	2	3			3	3
"	477	THOM Andrew	Mr	1		5	4	9		4	5	9
"	478	SMITH		1		2	5	7		1	6	7
"	479		'ARK'	11		10	13	23		21	2	23
"	480		'ARK'	9		3	12	15		9	6	15
"	481	MACDONALD	Mrs	1		2	3	5			5	5
"	482	WOOD Alexander		3		5	5	10		2	8	10
"	483	ROBERTSON Joseph		2		3	6	9		1	8	9
"	484	WALKER James		2		6	2	8		4	4	8
"	485	PROTT James		1	1	1		1		1		1
"	486	FERGUSON John		3		4	3	7			7	7
"	487	DUNCAN James		3		7	5	12		5	7	12
"	488	CLARK Thomas		4		3	7	10		2	8	10
"	489	PETRIE William		3		6	3	9		3	6	9
School-brae	490	HIRD John		1		2	3	9			5	5
"	491	TAYLOR Margaret		1			1	5			1	1
"	492	WEBSTER Elspet		1			1	1			1	1
"	493	DANIEL John		2		1	2	1			3	3
"	494	HAY George		3		6	10	3		6	10	16
"	495	THOM James		3		3	3	16		1	5	6
"	496	INNES Alexander		1		3	2	6		1	4	5
"	497	MILNE William		2		1	4	5		1	4	5
Maiden-Lane	498	BURNETT James		1		3	2	5		3	2	5
				67	2	91	113	204	5	74	130	204
				871	6	1259	1736	2995		648	2342	2995

Address	No. House	Name of Principal Tenant			Col 4	Col 5	Col 6	Col 7	Col 8	Col 9	Col 10	Col 11	Col 12
Maiden-Lane	499	STRACHAN	John		3		7	8	15		4	11	15
"	500	ABERNETHY		Mrs	2		2	4	6			6	6
"	501	ROSS	David		1		1	4	5			5	5
"	502	DANIEL	William		2		1	6	7			7	7
"	503	HANLAW		Mr	1		2	3	5			5	5
"	504	PIRIE	John		2	1	1	3	4			4	4
"	505	MARSHALL		Mrs	1		1	5	6			6	6
"	506	REID		Mr	1		1	2	3			3	3
"	507	PATON	John		2		1	3	4		1	3	4
Kirktown	508	MATTHEW	John		1		2	5	7		2	5	7
"	509	KING	Alexander		2		2	3	5		1	4	5
"	510	MITCHEL	William		2		1	1	2			2	2
"	511	SMITH	William		2		2	3	5			5	5
"	512	SCOTT	Alexander		1		3	6	9		1	8	9
"	513	DINNIS	John		1		3	1	4		2	2	4
"	514	KING	Charles		1		4	4	8		2	6	8
"	515	GLENNIE	James		1		1	1	2			2	2
"	516	SIEVEWRIGHT	William		1		3	2	5			5	5
"	517	HALL	Isabel		1			1	1			1	1
"	518	GORDON	Alexander		1		1	2	3			3	3
"	519	ROSS	John		1		2	1	3			3	3
"	520	SLICER	George		1		1	1	2		1	1	2
"	521	MILNE	Thomas		1		2	1	3		1	2	3
"	522	RAINIE	John		1		2	3	5		1	4	5
"	523	ROBB	William		1		3	3	6			6	6
"	524	BRUCE	Jean		2			2	2			2	2
"	525	OGSTON	John		2		3	5	8			8	8
"	526	FORGIE	John		2		3	3	6	2		4	6
"	527	HENDERSON	Jean		2			2	2			2	2
"	528	THOMSON	Andrew		1		1	1	2		1	1	2
					43	1	56	89	145	2	17	126	145
					914	7	1315	1825	3140	7	665	2468	3140

Page 21

Address	No. House	Name of Principal Tenant			Col 4	Col 5	Col 6	Col 7	Col 8	Col 9	Col 10	Col 11	Col 12
Kirktown	529	HUTTON	James		2		2	2	4	1	1	2	4
"	530	LIGERTWOOD	John		1		1	3	4		1	3	4
"	531	ANDERSON		Widow	1			1	1			1	1
"	532	CARNO	Robert		1		1	5	6	1		5	6
"	533	WILLOX	William		1		2	1	3		1	2	3
"	534	THOM	John		1		4	3	7	1		6	7
"	535	SMITH	Isabel		1			1	1			1	1
"	536	LUCKIE	Jean		1			1	1			1	1
"	537	GORDON	George		1		1	1	2			2	2
"	538	BURD		Mrs	1			3	3			3	3
"	539	FARQUHAR	William		2		3	3	6		1	5	6
"	540	YULE	James		2		3	2	5		2	3	5
"	541	YULE	John		2		6	5	11		2	9	11
"	542	MOIR		Dr.	1		2	5	7			7	7
"	543	FORBES	James		1		4	4	8		2	6	8
"	544	MORICE	William		1		2	3	5		2	3	5
"	545	LAW	William		4		5	6	11		2	9	11
"	546	THOMSON	George		1		10	3	13		9	4	13
"	547	FARQUHAR	Alexander		2		2	1	3		1	2	3
"	548	JACK	William		1		2	1	3		2	1	3
"	549	LESLIE	Robert		2		4	5	9		3	6	9
"	550	CATTO	James		2		2	2	4		1	3	4
"	551	HAY	James		1		3	4	7		1	6	7
					33	7	59	65	124	3	31	90	124
					947		1374	1890	3264	10	696	2558	3264

(Country Part of the Parish of Peterhead)

Address	No. House	Name of Principal Tenant			Col 4	Col 5	Col 6	Col 7	Col 8	Col 9	Col 10	Col 11	Col 12
Invernethie	1	OGSTON	John		2		8	4	12	4	3	5	12
"	2	CLARK	William (Meethill)		1		2	2	4	4			4
"	3	CLARK	William (Mills)		1		3	3	6	5		1	6
"	4	LAWRIE	William		1		1	2	3	2	1		3
"	5	LAWRIE	George		1		2	3	5	1	1	3	5
"	6	ROBERTSON	John		1		5	3	8	7		1	8
"	7	EWEN	David		2		1	3	4	2	1	1	4
"	8	CHALMERS	Charles		1		2		2	2			2
"	9	DUNCAN	John		2		1	5	6	2		4	6
"	10	MILNE	Andrew		1		2	2	4	2	1	1	4
"	11	GORDON		Mr	1		3	3	6	6			6
"	12	FORBES	James	Junior	1		4	2	6	4		2	6
"	13	WOOD	Alexander		1		6	4	10	4	1	5	10
"	14	KIDD	Alexander		1		3	4	7	2		5	7
Invernethie Lodge	15	OGSTON	John		1		3	2	5	3		2	5
"	16	RAMSAY		Major	1		1	1	2			2	2
"	17	STEVENSON	James		1		2	3	5	3		2	5
"	18	LAWRENCE	Thomas		1		3	4	7	4		3	7
"	19	HUTTON	George		2		2	3	5	2	1	2	5
"	20	BROOK	James		1		1	1	2	2			2
"	21	ROBERTSON	James		1		2	3	5		2	3	5
"	22	ROBERTSON	James		1		1	2	3	3			3
"	23	PETRIE	Margaret		1		1	1	2	3			2
"	24	GREIG	Margaret		1			2	2	2			2
"	25	LUCKIE	Sarah		1		1	2	3		2	2	3
"	26	DUFF	James		1		1	3	4		1	1	4
"	27	ELRICK	Alexander		1		6	3	9	8		3	9
"	28	GILLIES	William		1		1	2	3	2	1	1	3
"	29	ABERNETHIE	John		1		1	2	3	3			3
"	30	ROBERTSON	John		1		3	4	7	7			7
					34		72	78	150	86	15	49	150

Address	No. House	Name of Principal Tenant			Col 4	Col 5	Col 6	Col 7	Col 8	Col 9	Col 10	Col 11	Col 12
Invernethie	31	SMITH	John		1		2	5	7	4		3	7
Lodge	32	ROBERTSON	Thomas		1		4	2	6	6		3	6
Boddam	33	BROCKIE	Charles		1		1	1	2	2			2
"	34	MITCHEL	John		1		3	1	4	4			4
"	35	MITCHEL	James		1		2	2	4	2		2	4
"	36	LAWRIE	Alexander		2		2	3	5	4		1	5
"	37	SCOTT	James		1		2	3	5	2		2	5
"	38	SANGSTER	James		1		2	5	7	4	1	3	7
"	39	GREIG	James		1		2	3	5	4		1	5
"	40	LAW	William		1		1	3	4	1		3	4
"	41	MITCHEL	Alexander		1		3	4	7	6		1	7
"	42	LEMON	John		1		2	3	5	3		2	5
"	43	CLARK	James		1		3	6	9	7		2	9
"	44	ALEXANDER	John		1		1	3	4	2		2	4
"	45	ROBERTSON	Thomas		1		1	2	3		1	2	3
"	46	ELRICK	William		1		2	2	4	1	1	2	4
"	47	DANIEL	Isabel		1		3	1	4	2		2	4
"	48	HAY	William		1		3	1	4	4			4
"	49	SANGSTER	George		1		2	4	6	3		3	6
"	50	BARCLAY	James		1		3	2	5	2		3	5
"	51	LAW	Alexander		2		1	2	3	3			3
"	52	BRUCE	Alexander		1		2	3	5		1	4	5
"	53	SCOTT	John		1		3	2	5		1	4	5
"	54	MILNE	William		1		1	1	2	2			2
"	55	GRAY	George		1		1	1	2	2			2
"	56	ROBERTSON	George	Widow	2		4	4	8			8	8
"	57	MACDONALD	James		1		2	2	4	2		2	4
Town of Boddam	58	MACKIE	George		1		2	4	6		6		6
" "	59	TAYLOR	Mary		1			1	1			1	1
" "	60	BRUCE	Margaret		1			1	1			1	1
					33		60	77	137	72	11	54	137
					67		132	155	287	158	26	103	287

Address	No. House	Name of Principal Tenant		Col 4	Col 5	Col 6	Col 7	Col 8	Col 9	Col 10	Col 11	Col 12
Town of Boddam	61	BRUCE	William	2		3	2	5		3	2	5
" "	62	SELLER	William	1		4	4	8		6	2	8
" "	63	CORDINER	Robert	1		1	4	5		2	3	5
" "	64	HUTCHEON	George	1		1	1	2		2		2
" "	65	HUTCHEON	John	1		2	2	4		2	2	4
" "	66	CORDINER	William	1		4	3	7		3	4	7
" "	67	TAYLOR	Janet	1		3	3	6		6		6
" "	68	CORDINER	Alexander	1		1	2	3		2	1	3
" "	69	HUTCHEON	Jean	1		2	3	5		4	1	5
" "	70	SOUTTER	Jean	1			1	1			1	1
" "	71	STEPHEN	William	1		1	1	2		2		2
" "	72	STEPHEN	William	1		4	1	5		4	1	5
" "	73	BRUCE	George	1		2	2	4		2	2	4
" "	74	BROWN	William	1		4	2	6		6		6
" "	75	MACKIE	Mary	1			1	1			1	1
" "	76	STEPHEN	George	1		1	1	2		1	1	2
" "	77	STEPHEN	John	1		4	5	9		6	3	9
" "	78	TAYLOR	James	1		1	2	3		3		3
" "	79	CORDINER	Alexander	1		5	3	8		8		8
" "	80	SELLER	John	1		4	5	9		7		9
" "	81	SELLER	Mary	1			1	1				1
" "	82	HUTCHEON	George	1		3	3	6		5	1	6
" "	83	TAYLOR	Alexander	1		3	4	7		3	4	7
" "	84	BRUCE	Alexander	1		2	3	5		4	1	5
" "	85	TAYLOR	Jean	1		1	4	5			5	5
" "	86	STEPHEN	Robert	1		2	1	3		3		3
" "	87	HUTCHEON	Alexander	1		1	2	3		2	1	3
" "	88	HUTCHEON	Alexander	1		1	3	4		4		4
" "	89	BRUCE	William	1		1	1	2		2		2
" "	90	HUTCHEON	William	1		3	3	6		4	2	6
				31		64	73	137		96	41	137
				98		196	228	424	158	122	144	424

Address	No. House	Name of Principal Tenant		Col 4	Col 5	Col 6	Col 7	Col 8	Col 9	Col 10	Col 11	Col 12
Town of Boddam	91	STEPHEN	William	1		3	2	5		2	3	5
" "	92	TAYLOR	Marjory	1			2	2			2	2
" "	93	BROWN	James	1		1	1	2				2
" "	94	STEPHEN	George	1		3	2	5		2	3	5
" "	95	STEPHEN	Robert	1		4	1	5		2	3	5
" "	96	MACKIE	Margaret	1			3	3		3		3
" "	97	STEPHEN	Robert	1		2	3	5		2	3	5
" "	98	STEPHEN	Alexander	1		1	1	2		2		2
" "	99	STEPHEN	William	1		3	2	5		2	3	5
" "	100	HUTCHEON	John	1		1	3	4		4		4
" "	101	ROBB	Mary	1		1	2	3		2	1	3
" "	102	STEPHEN	William	1		1	1	2		2		2
" "	103	HUTCHEON	George	1		4	2	6		4	2	6
" "	104	ROBB	Elspet	1			1	1			1	1
" "	105	HUTCHEON	Christian	1		1	2	3		2	1	3
" "	106	STEPHEN	Margaret	1			1	1			1	1
Little Cocklaw	107	OGSTON	Marjory	1			1	1			1	1
" "	108	MURISON	Alexander	1		3	1	4	2		2	4
" "	109	BROOK	James	1		2	1	3	1			3
" "	110	WEBSTER	John	1		1	2	3	3	2		3
" "	111	JOHNSTON	Peter	1		1	1	2	2			2
" "	112	MURISON	George	1		5	4	9	4		5	9
" "	113	CHEYNE	Elspet	1			2	2	2			2
" "	114	MATHERS	James	1		2	3	5	2		3	5
" "	115	GALL	James	1		2	2	4	3	1		4
" "	116	FORRESTER	Mrs	1			7	7			7	7
" "	117	SAMUEL	Andrew	1		1	1	2	2			2
" "	118	JACK	Jean	1			1	1			1	1
" "	119	LOGAN	William	1		1	3	4	3		1	4
" "	120	CROOKSHANK	William	1		3	1	4	3		1	4
				30	0	46	59	105	27	34	44	105
				128	0	242	287	529	185	156	188	529

Address	No. House	Name of Principal Tenant			Col 4	Col 5	Col 6	Col 7	Col 8	Col 9	Col 10	Col 11	Col 12
Little Cocklaw	121	MUTCH	James		1		3	5	8	5		3	8
"	122	WALKER	William		1		2	3	5	1	1	3	5
"	123	WHITECROSS	John		1		2	2	4	3		1	4
"	124	BEADIE	James		1		1	1	2	2			2
"	125	MILNE	John		1		2	2	4	3		1	4
"	126	OLDMAN	Gilbert		1		1	1	2	2			2
"	127	NICHOLSON	Mary		1			1	1	1			1
Collilaw	128	BEADIE	Isabel		1			2	2				2
"	129	WALKER	John		1		2	3	5	3	2		5
"	130	FALCONER	William		1		1	3	4	4	1	1	4
"	131	ROBERTSON	Christian		1			1	1			1	1
"	132	LAING	William		1		8	6	14	8		6	14
"	133	ALEXANDER	Elspet		1			1	1		1		1
"	134	MITCHEL	Robert		1		2	2	4	4			4
"	135	ROBERTSON	James		1		1		1				1
"	136	HAY	George		1		1	2	3	3		1	3
"	137	HAY	George	Junior	1		1	1	2		1	1	2
"	138	MURRAY	Thomas		1		2	4	6	2		4	6
Aughtigall	139	BEADIE	George		1		2	1	3	3			3
"	140	SANGSTER	William		1		5	1	6		1	5	6
"	141	WALLACE	James		1		2	2	4	2	1	1	4
"	142	WHITECROSS	Margaret		1		1	2	3			3	3
"	143	GEDDES	John		1		3	1	4	2		2	4
"	144	CROOKSHANK	Alexander		1		3	4	7	7			7
"	145	PATERSON	John		1		2	1	3	3			3
"	146	HAY	James		1		4	2	6	3		3	6
"	147	SIMPSON	Isabel		1			1	1	1		1	1
"	148	SHEWAN	Andrew		2		5	6	11	6		5	11
"	149	EWEN	John		1		3	3	6	3	3		6
"	150	OLDMAN	Alexander		1		3	3	6	2	1	3	6
					31	0	62	67	129	72	12	45	129
					159	0	304	354	658	257	168	233	658

Page 27

Address	No. House	Name of Principal Tenant		Col 4	Col 5	Col 6	Col 7	Col 8	Col 9	Col 10	Col 11	Col 12
Aughtigall	151	BRUCE	William	1				1			1	1
"	152	BRUCE	John	1		1		1	1			1
"	153	MILNE	Jean	2			2	2			2	2
Dens	154	MITCHEL	William	1		1	1	2				2
"	155	BODDIE	Elspet	1			4	4	2		4	4
"	156	GRANT	James	1		1	2	3	3			3
"	157	HAY	John	1		1	1	2	2			2
"	158	BEGRIE	Peter	1		2	4	6	2		4	6
"	159	BEGRIE	William	1		1		1			1	1
"	160	CROOKSHANK	James	1		3	4	7	4		3	7
"	161	CROOKSHANK	Barbara	1			3	3			3	3
"	162	MAITLAND	Adam	1		1	2	3	3			3
Thaws/Haws	163	ARBUTHNOT	William	1		4	1	5	5			5
"	164	HAY	James	1		2	2	4	2		2	4
"	165	REID	Alexander	1		2	3	5	5			5
"	166	CLARK	Alexander	1		2	3	5	2		3	5
"	167	STEPHEN	Christian	1			1	1			1	1
Mickle Cocklaw	168	GREIG	John	1		1	3	4	1	1	2	4
"	169	SMITH	Alexander	1		1	1	2	2			2
"	170	MILNE	George	1		1	1	2	2			2
"	171	SANDIE	James	1		5	3	8	1		7	8
"	172	OGSTON	Alexander	1		1	2	3		1	2	3
"	173	ROBERTSON	William	1		2	2	4			4	4
"	174	FRASER	Mary	1			1	1			1	1
"	175	RICHARD	James	1		1	3	4	3		1	4
"	176	THOMSON	Alexander	1		4	3	7	2	1	4	7
"	177	RICHARD	John	1		1	2	3	3			3
"	178	MACLEOD	William	1		1	1	2	2			2
"	179	GRANT	Widow			2	3	5	2		3	5
"	180	CRUDEN	James	1		3	4	7	5		2	7
				31	0	45	62	107	54	3	50	107
				190	0	349	416	765	311	171	283	765

Address	No. House	Name of Principal Tenant		Col 4	Col 5	Col 6	Col 7	Col 8	Col 9	Col 10	Col 11	Col 12
Mickle Cocklaw	181	LUCKIE	James	1		2	2	4	2	1	1	4
"	182	BARRON	James	1		1	4	5	2	1	2	5
"	183	SHIVES	Robert	1		1	2	3	3			3
"	184	MITCHEL	Widow	1		2	4	6	6			6
"	185	MITCHEL	William	1		2	2	4	4			4
"	186	BOYS	William	1		3	2	5	4		1	5
"	187	CLARK	Arthur	1		1	1	2	2			2
Downiehills	188	SKENE	Alexander	1		1	3	4	3		1	4
"	189	FORGIE	James	1		3	2	5	3		2	5
"	190	NICHOLSON	John	1		5	4	9	7		2	9
Glendavenie	191	WEBSTER	William	1		3	3	6	5		1	6
Smithy-hill	192	TAYLOR	Alexander	1		2	4	6	3		3	6
"	193	SCOTT	John	1		1	3	4	4			4
"	194	PIRIE	William	1		1	2	3	3			3
"	195	PARK	William	1		6	7	13	7		6	13
Torterstown	196	KIDD	John	1		4	1	5	5			5
Newseat	197	KIDD	James	1		6	4	10	10			10
"	198	SUMMERS	Robert	1		4	2	6	2		4	6
Barnyards	199	GREIG	James	1		3	5	8	8			8
"	200	KIDD	William	1		4	6	10	8		2	10
"	201	LILLIE	Widow	1			2	2			2	2
"	202	JOHNSTON	William	1		1	2	3	3			3
"	203	ANNAND	Alexander	1		1	4	5	2		3	5
"	204	MESS	George	1		5	4	9	9			9
"	205	MESS	Barbara	1			1	1				1
Rosefield	206	HUTTON	John	1		3	2	5	2	2	1	5
"	207	CROOKSHANK	Alexander	1		1	4	5		3	2	5
"	208	CRIGHTON	George	1		2	2	4		1	3	4
"	209	TAYLOR	Andrew	1		3	2	5		1	4	5
"	210	PATERSON	Alexander	1		2	1	3		1	2	3
				30	0	73	87	160	107	10	43	160
				220		422	503	925	418	181	326	925

Address	No. House	Name of Principal Tenant	Col 4	Col 5	Col 6	Col 7	Col 8	Col 9	Col 10	Col 11	Col 12
Scotsmill	211	LILLIE William	1		3	4	7	4		3	7
"	212	CHRISTIE William	1		1	1	2		2		2
"	213	WILL Peter	1			2	2			2	2
"	214	REID (Widow)	1		1	1	2			2	2
"	215	ARGO George	1		3	2	5	4		1	5
"	216	BAIRD John	1		2	2	4	4			4
"	217	BAIRD William	1		3	2	5	3		2	5
Mickle Cocklaw	218	JAMIESON William	1		3	3	6	6			6
Mount Pleasant	219	SIM William (Mr)	1		3	6	9	7		2	9
"	220	URQUHART John	1		1	2	3	3			3
Hayfield	221	HUTCHISON John (Capt'n)	1		2	2	4	4			4
Balmoor	222	CASSIE Robert	1		3	4	7	3		4	7
"	223	HADDEN William	1		1	4	5	2	1	2	5
"	224	HADDEN Robert	1		2	3	5	2	1	2	5
"	225	SMITH James	1		3	5	8	3		5	8
"	226	MASON George	1		2	3	5	5			5
"	227	MASON William	1		1	2	3	2		1	3
"	228	MESS William	1		3	3	6	2			6
"	229	OLDMAN George	1		2	2	4	4		4	4
"	230	TURRIFF David	1		1	2	3	3			3
"	231	OGILVIE Alexander	1		2	4	6	2			6
Clarkhill	232	BERRY William	1		2	2	4		2	4	4
"	233	ELLIS William (Capt'n)	1		2	1	3	3		2	3
"	234	CRAIG James	1		1	4	5	4			5
"	235	JAFFRAY William	1		1	1	2	2		1	2
"	236	ANNAND John	1		1	2	3	1	1		3
"	237	CLARK John	1		4	4	8	4		1	8
"	238	ANGUS Alexander	1		2	2	4	3		4	4
"	239	EWEN Alexander (Widow)	1		2	3	5	3	2	1	5
"	240	EWEN James	1		1	3	4		1	3	4
			30	0	58	81	139	83	10	46	139
			250	0	480	584	1064	501	191	372	1064

Address	No. House	Name of Principal Tenant			Col 4	Col 5	Col 6	Col 7	Col 8	Col 9	Col 10	Col 11	Col 12
Clarkhill	241	FORGIE	William		1		4	2	6	3		3	6
"	242	DAVIDSON		Widow	1		3	2	5	2	1	2	5
"	243	FINDLAY	James		1		1	2	3	2		1	3
Grange	244	SHEWAN	Robert		1		1	1	2			2	2
"	245	MITCHELL	William		1		4	4	8	4		4	8
"	246	JAFFRAY	Andrew		1		2	6	8	3		5	8
"	247	OGSTON	William		1		2	5	7	4		3	7
"	248	PIRIE	James		1		1	4	5			2	5
"	249	JOHNSTON	Alexander		1		5	5	10	1	3	2	10
"	250	ROBB	John		1		2	3	5	3	7	2	5
"	251	SMITH	William		1		3	3	6	6			6
"	252	SLICER	Alexander		1	1	1		1	1			1
Blackhouse	253	SHIVES	Robert		1		2	1	3	3			3
"	254	JOHNSTON	Alexander		1		2	1	3	3			3
"	255	COPLAND	John		1		2	1	3	3			3
"	256	JOHNSTON	James		1		4	3	7	4	1	2	7
"	257	SAMUEL	Robert		1		2	2	4	4			4
"	258	GOW	Alexander		1		2	3	5	3		2	5
"	259	FARQUHAR	Margaret		1			1	1			1	1
"	260	BRANDS	Alexander		1		2	2	4	4			4
"	261	REID		Mr	1		4	6	10	7		3	10
Buchan-Haven	262	CHRISTIE	William		3		1	6	7		5	2	7
"	263	GRAY	James		1		1	3	4	2		2	4
"	264	ALLARDYCE	William		1		4	1	5		1	4	5
"	265	GRAY	Margaret		1			1	1			1	1
"	266	GREIG	Alexander		1		2	1	3	1		2	3
"	267	JOHNSTON	William		1		2	1	3		1	2	3
"	268	WALLACE	John		1		3		3		3		3
"	269	CATTO	David		1		1	1	2	1	1		2
"	270	STRACHAN	John		1		3	2	5		1	4	5
					32	1	66	73	139	64	24	51	139
					282	1	546	657	1203	565	215	423	1203

Address	No. House	Name of Principal Tenant		Col 4	Col 5	Col 6	Col 7	Col 8	Col 9	Col 10	Col 11	Col 12
Buchan-Haven	271	DAVIDSON	Alexander	1		3	2	5	2		3	5
" "	272	STUART	Charles	1		3	3	6		2	4	6
" "	273	DUGUID	John	1		1	2	3			3	3
Wind-Mill	274	COWIE	William	1		3	2	5	2		3	5
Washing-House	275	MURISON	William	1		3	2	5	4	1	3	5
				5		13	11	24	8	3	13	24
	275	*Country Part of Peterhead*		287	1	559	668	1227	573	218	436	1227
	551	*Town of Peterhead*		947	7	1374	1890	3264	10	696	2558	3264
	826	*Whole Parish of Peterhead*		1234	8	1933	2558	4491	583	914	2994	4491

N.B. The Fourth Question requires the Numbers of Males and Females baptized, and of Burials, in the several Years under-mentioned; 'nd the Fifth Question the Number of Marriages in the several Years from 1; '4 to 1800 inclusively.

Baptisms.

Years	Male	Female	Total
1700	28	12	40
1710	39	44	83
1720	43	29	72
1730	19	17	36
1740	18	21	39
1750	13	13	26
1760	17	15	32
1770	23	20	43
1780	10	12	22
1781	11	11	22
1782	9	12	21
1783	10	9	19
1784	8	11	19
1785	9	10	19
1786	17	7	24
1787	8	10	18
1788	8	7	15
1789	16	9	25
1790	9	6	15
1791	12	11	23
1792	10	5	15
1793	10	9	19

1794

1794	13	7	20
1795	13	6	19
1796	11	14	25
1797	11	6	17
1798	12	10	22
1799	6	9	15
1800	14	7	21

Marriages

1754	13
1755	20
1756	19
1758	15
1759	16
1760	14
1761	13
1762	11
1763	16
1799	25
1800	26

REMARKS, in Explanation of the Answers, agreeably to the Sixth Question.

First three question. As the Parish of Peterhead consists of a town and Tract of Country adjoining to it, the several Particulars in Answer to the first Questions are given for the Town and Country Part separately, and then for the Parish together.

First Question. In the Number of Inhabited Houses are not included (Separate Manufacturing-Houses and Shops: of these there are 118 in the Town of Peterhead, and 28 in the Country Part of the Parish; in all 146.

Fourth Question. The Registration of Baptisms has been so much neglected by the Parents in this Parish, that the Register cannot at all be depended on regard to the Number of Baptisms, especially in the later years. No Register of Burials has been kept for a Century past in this Parish.
Fifth Question. No Register of Marriages has been kept in this Parish for the Period specified in the Question, except in the Years stated above.

STATEMENT of the PROGRESSIVE POPULATION of PETERHEAD

In 1764 the Number of Males in the Town of Peterhead was 530; and of Females 736: total 1266. In the Country Part of the Parish the Males were 553; and the Females 601: total 1154. Total in the Parish 2420. - In 1769 the Males in the Town were 640; and the Females 878: total 1518. In the Country the Males were 589; and the Females 599: total 1188 Total in the Parish 2706. - In 1790 there were in the Town 1097 Males; and 1453 Females: in all 2550. - In 1794 there were in the Country 518 Males; and 623 Females: in all 1141. - In the present year (1801) the Males in the Town of Peterhead are 1374; and the Females 1890: total 3264. In the country Part of the Parish the Males are 559; and the Females 668: total 1227. In the whole Parish there are at present 1933 Males; and 2558 Females: in all 4491.

Omitted in the foregoing Statement

By an Account taken by Dr. Moir, Minister of Peterhead in the year 1800, the number of Inhabitants in the Town of Peterhead was 3169, and in the Country Part of the Parish 1202; in all 4371. Of these there were above twelve years of age 2341 in the Town, and 864 in the Country; in all 3205. There were in the town 2215 Presbyterians the Established Church, and in the Country 980; in all And of Presbyterians above twelve ther were in the town 1572, in the country 712; in all 2284.

This and the preceding Statement are certified

George Moir   Minister
A. Adamson   Session-Clerk

AN IMPRESSION OF
The Town and Parish of PETERHEAD around 1801

St. Fergus Parish

NORTH

Rosefield

Newseat

Scotsmill

Barnyards

Balmoor

Torterstown

Mount Pleasant

Glendavinie

Smithyhill

Buchan Haven

Blackhouse

Wind Mill

Downiehills

Hayfield

Howe O' Buchan

Washing House

Longside Parish

Grange

Kirktown

SEE TOWN MAP

Clarkhill

Little Cocklaw

Hillhead of Cocklaw

Meethill

Dens

I. Lodge

Inverneftie

Auchtiegall

North

Collilaw

South

Mountpleasant

Town of Boddam

Cruden Parish

PETERHEAD

PETERHEAD BAY

THESE MAPS ARE BASED UPON ROBERTSON'S MAP OF 1822
& ROY'S MAP OF 1750. OTHER PLACE-NAMES HAVE BEEN
ADDED FROM VARIOUS WRITTEN SOURCES AND LOCAL
KNOWLEDGE

HOW A DOCUMENT LIKE THIS TURNS UP

The appearance of an 1801 document in the 1990's makes people ask, "Where has it been all this time?"

Items like this usually turn up in a collection of material that has not been properly identified, listed, or catalogued, and may appear from estate papers, church records, local authority records, museums, libraries and archives of all types.

This particular document was found quite a few years ago in the safe at Peterhead Library, and the librarian at the time and now retired, George Brebner, tells me that it was there since before his tenure and that probably it had been given to the Peterhead Burgh Library some time soon after the library was opened in the 1890's.

The library in its early days, like many others, did not have any demand for such material, and instead took upon itself the admirable duty of preservation for the future.

Some time after local government reorganisation, unique local history items were centralised to the new N.E. Scotland Library Service headquarters at Oldmeldrum, and placed in a fire-proof store. A photocopy was made available to allow indexing and publication as you now see it.

If you hear of any similar items that are not recorded, please let us know so that we can investigate further.

North-East Scotland Service,
Meldrum Meg Way,
The Meadows Industrial Estate,
Oldmeldrum,
Aberdeenshire.

INDEX

Surname	Chr.Names	Title	Page	Surname	Chr.Names	Title	Page
BURNETT	Alexander		2	CRAIGHEAD	James		4
BURNETT	James		19	CRAWFORD	Charles		2
BUTTER	James		12	CRIGHTON	Alexander		15
CAIRD	Anne		14	CRIGHTON	George		28
CAMPBELL	Alex'r		15	CROOKSHANK	Alexander		26
CAMPBELL	James		15	CROOKSHANK	Alexander		28
CARNO	Robert		21	CROOKSHANK	Barbara		27
CASSIE	Robert		29	CROOKSHANK	James		27
CATTO	Charles		7	CROOKSHANK	John		17
CATTO	David		30	CROOKSHANK	John		12
CATTO	James		21	CROOKSHANK	William		25
CHALMERS	Charles		22	CROOKSHANK	William		15
CHALMERS	Robert		7	CRUDEN	James		27
CHEYNE		Mrs	3	CUMINE	Alexander		16
CHEYNE	Elspet		25	CUMINE	Charles		4
CHEYNE	James		11	DALGARNO		Mrs	6
CHEYNE	John		8	DALLACHY	John		6
CHEYNE	Thomas		16	DALRYMPLE	Robert		16
CHEYNE	William		14	DANIEL	Andrew		2
CHISHOLM	John		9	DANIEL	Isabel		23
CHRISTIE	Alexander		6	DANIEL	John		19
CHRISTIE	Margaret		16	DANIEL	William		20
CHRISTIE	William		29	DARG	Andrew		16
CHRISTIE	William		30	DAVIDSON		Widow	30
CLACKIE	George		2	DAVIDSON		Mrs	13
CLARK	Alexander		7	DAVIDSON		Mrs	8
CLARK	Alexander		12	DAVIDSON	Alexander		31
CLARK	Alexander		27	DAVIDSON	Alexander		12
CLARK	Arthur		28	DAVIDSON	Andrew		4
CLARK	David		7	DAVIDSON	Christian		12
CLARK	James		10	DAVIDSON	John		4
CLARK	James		23	DAVIDSON	John		11
CLARK	John		18	DAVIDSON	Thomas		4
CLARK	John		29	DAVIDSON	William		18
CLARK	Thomas		19	DAVIDSON	William		5
CLARK	Wm, Meethill		22	DAVIDSON	William		16
				DAWSON		Mrs	9
CLARK	Wm, Mills		22	DINNET	John		13
				DINNIES	John		10
CLOCKIE	George		6	DINNIS	John		20
COGLAN			4	DUFF	James		22
CONNAN	Alexander		5	DUGUID	John		31
COPLAND	John		30	DUN	Elisabeth		13
CORDINER		Mrs	6	DUN	Janet		13
CORDINER	Alexander		24	DUN	Robert		13
CORDINER	Alexander		24	DUNBAR	Peter		12
CORDINER	Elspet		13	DUNBAR	Rob't		15
CORDINER	James		13	DUNCAN		Mrs	14
CORDINER	Robert		24	DUNCAN		Widow	13
CORDINER	William		24	DUNCAN	Alexander		13
CORMACK		Widow	13	DUNCAN	Charles		6
CORMACK	George		8	DUNCAN	James		19
CORMACK	Janet		14	DUNCAN	John		22
CORMACK	William		14	DUNCAN	John		3
COWIE	William		31	DUNCAN	Margaret		6
CRAIG	Alexander		18	ELLES		Capt'n	7
CRAIG	James		29	ELLIS		Capt'n	29

Surname	Chr.Names	Title	Page	Surname	Chr.Names	Title	Page
ELRICK	Alexander		22	GIBSON	William		7
ELRICK	William		23	GILLIE	John		18
EWEN		Widow	29	GILLIES	William		22
EWEN	David		22	GLENNIE	James		20
EWEN	James		29	GORDON		Mrs	10
EWEN	John		26	GORDON		Mr	22
FALCONER	William		26	GORDON	Alexander		9
FARQUHAR	Alexander		21	GORDON	Alexander		20
FARQUHAR	James		15	GORDON	George		21
FARQUHAR	Margaret		30	GORDON	James		7
FARQUHAR	William		21	GORDON	John		8
FARQUHAR	William		18	GOW	Alexander		30
FERGUSON		Capt'n	16	GRANT		Widow	27
FERGUSON	George		11	GRANT	Isabel		14
FERGUSON	John		19	GRANT	James		27
FINDLATER	John		17	GRANT	John		18
FINDLATER	William		9	GRANT	Patrick		15
FINDLAY		Mrs	5	GRAY	Elisabeth		10
FINDLAY	James		30	GRAY	George		23
FORBES		Mr	17	GRAY	George		7
FORBES		Mrs	18	GRAY	Isabel		12
FORBES		Mrs	17	GRAY	James		30
FORBES	Alexander		18	GRAY	James		14
FORBES	Andrew		5	GRAY	Janet		12
FORBES	James		6	GRAY	John		11
FORBES	James		10	GRAY	Margaret		30
FORBES	James	Junior	3	GREGORY	John		10
FORBES	James		21	GREIG	Alexander		30
FORBES	James	Junior	22	GREIG	Alexander		10
FORBES	Thomas		15	GREIG	James		28
FORGIE	James		28	GREIG	James		23
FORGIE	John		20	GREIG	John		27
FORGIE	William		30	GREIG	Margaret		22
FORREST	Alexander		11	HACKET	William		10
FORREST	James		15	HADDEN	Robert		29
FORREST	Peter		7	HADDEN	William		29
FORREST	Thomas		4	HALL	Isabel		20
FORREST	William		15	HANLAW		Mr	20
FORRESTER		Mrs	25	HARVEY		Mr	16
FORSYTH	John		5	HAY	George		19
FRASER		Mrs	16	HAY	George	Junior	26
FRASER		Mrs	6	HAY	George		26
FRASER	Donald		15	HAY	James		26
FRASER	James		5	HAY	James		21
FRASER	Mary		27	HAY	James		27
FYFE	Charles		15	HAY	John		27
FYFE	Charles		11	HAY	Robert		18
GALL	Alexander		14	HAY	Robert		8
GALL	James		25	HAY	Thomas		11
GALLOWAY		Mrs	16	HAY	William		23
GARDEN	George		16	HAY	William		18
GARDEN	John		6	HECTOR	Elspet		6
GEDDES	John		26	HENDERSON	Jean		20
GERRIE	Alexander		13	HENDERSON	Patrick		6
GERRIE	John		9	HENDERSON	Robert		2
GERRIE	Robert		13	HIRD	John		19
GIBB	Robert		4	HIRD	John		7

Surname	Chr.Names	Title	Page	Surname	Chr.Names	Title	Page
HOWIE	William		18	KIDD	William		28
HUNTER		Mrs	3	KIER	Mary		10
HURRIE	Gilbert		16	KILGOUR		Mrs	3
HUTCHEON	Alexander		24	KING	Alexander		20
HUTCHEON	Alexander		24	KING	Charles		20
HUTCHEON	Christian		25	KING	James		2
HUTCHEON	George		24	KNOX	Andrew		11
HUTCHEON	George		25	LAING		Dr	5
HUTCHEON	George		24	LAING	William		26
HUTCHEON	Jean		24	LAMB		Mrs	2
HUTCHEON	John		25	LAW	Alexander		23
HUTCHEON	John		24	LAW	William		21
HUTCHEON	William		24	LAW	William		23
HUTCHISON		Capt'n	19	LAWRENCE	George		14
HUTCHISON		Capt'n	29	LAWRENCE	Thomas		22
HUTCHISON		Mrs	10	LAWRIE	Alexander		23
HUTCHISON		Capt'n	2	LAWRIE	George		22
HUTCHISON		Mr	2	LAWRIE	William		22
HUTCHISON	George		12	LAWSON	William		8
HUTCHISON	George		16	LEASK	James		13
HUTCHISON	James		4	LEASK	William		6
HUTCHISON	James		4	LEITH	John		18
HUTCHISON	Janet		11	LEMON	John		23
HUTCHISON	John		10	LESLIE	John		17
HUTTON	George		22	LESLIE	Robert		21
HUTTON	James		21	LIBERTY		Mrs	5
HUTTON	John		28	LIGERTWOOD	John		21
IMLAY	James		7	LILLIE		Widow	28
INNES	Alexander		19	LILLIE	William		29
IRONSIDE	John		19	LILLIE	William		12
JACK	Jean		25	LIND		Mrs	9
JACK	Lewis		14	LIVINGSTONE		Mrs	3
JACK	Thomas		7	LOGAN	William		25
JACK	William		17	LORIMER	George		11
JACK	William		21	LOW	James		11
JAFFRAY		Mrs	18	LOW	Mary		2
JAFFRAY	Andrew		30	LUCKIE	James		28
JAFFRAY	James		6	LUCKIE	Jean		21
JAFFRAY	John		17	LUCKIE	Sarah		22
JAFFRAY	William		29	LYON	Andrew		6
JAMIESON		Dr.	18	LYON	George		5
JAMIESON	William		29	MACDONALD		Mrs	19
JOHNSTON	Alexander		30	MACDONALD	James		23
JOHNSTON	Alexander		30	MACDONALD	Kenneth		16
JOHNSTON	James		30	MACDONALD	William		8
JOHNSTON	James		18	MACGILLAVRY	Robert		12
JOHNSTON	Peter		25	MACINTOSH		Capt'n	7
JOHNSTON	William		30	MACKENZIE	Calib		12
JOHNSTON	William		28	MACKENZIE	Isabel		9
KAY		Mrs	3	MACKENZIE	John		16
KEIR	Robert		5	MACKIE		Mrs	9
KEITH		Mrs	14	MACKIE	Alexander		9
KEITH	Alexander		13	MACKIE	Alexander		7
KEITH	George		4	MACKIE	George		23
KIDD	Alexander		22	MACKIE	John		13
KIDD	James		28	MACKIE	Margaret		25
KIDD	John		28	MACKIE	Mary		24

Surname	Chr.Names	Title	Page	Surname	Chr.Names	Title	Page
MACKIE	William		13	MOIR		Dr.	21
MACLALLEAN	John		10	MOIR	Jean		8
MACLEAN		Mrs	4	MOIR	John		9
MACLEOD	William		27	MORICE	James		9
MACPHERSON	John		15	MORICE	William		21
MAIN	Robert		8	MORISON	George		14
MAITLAND	Adam		16	MORISON	Joseph		4
MAITLAND	Adam		27	MORRICE	John		2
MARSHALL		Mrs	20	MOWAT		Mrs	16
MASON	George		29	MURDOCH	John		13
MASON	William		29	MURISON	Alexander		25
MATHERS	James		25	MURISON	George		15
MATTHEW		Mrs	17	MURISON	George		25
MATTHEW	Alexander		17	MURISON	Marjory		11
MATTHEW	George		15	Murison	William		31
MATTHEW	George		8	MURRAY	Hugh		11
MATTHEW	James		7	MURRAY	Thomas		26
MATTHEW	John		20	MUTCH	Barbara		5
MATTHEW	Thomas		5	MUTCH	George		8
MAVOR	George		4	MUTCH	James		26
MESS	Barbara		28	MUTCH	John		4
MESS	Christian		6	MUTCH	Katharine		5
MESS	George		28	MUTCHISON	George		12
MESS	William		29	NEDDRIE	Charles		5
MILNE		Mr	5	NICHOLSON	John		28
MILNE	Andrew		22	NICHOLSON	Mary		26
MILNE	Christian		13	OGILVIE	Alexander		6
MILNE	George		14	OGILVIE	Alexander		29
MILNE	George		27	OGSTON	Alexander		27
MILNE	George		2	OGSTON	George		5
MILNE	Isabel		4	OGSTON	John		22
MILNE	Isabel		5	OGSTON	John		22
MILNE	James		14	OGSTON	John		20
MILNE	James		18	OGSTON	Marjory		25
MILNE	Jean		27	OGSTON	Robert		2
MILNE	John		3	OGSTON	William		30
MILNE	John		26	OLDMAN	Alexander		26
MILNE	Margaret		15	OLDMAN	George		29
MILNE	Thomas		20	OLDMAN	Gilbert		26
MILNE	William		15	PARK	William		28
MILNE	William		19	PARKS		Misses	17
MILNE	William		23	PARKS		Misses	17
MINTO		Widow	14	PATERSON	Alexander		28
MITCHEL		Widow	28	PATERSON	John		16
MITCHEL	Alexander		23	PATERSON	John		26
MITCHEL	Charles		9	PATERSON	William		17
MITCHEL	James		23	PATON	John		20
MITCHEL	James		10	PETRIE		Miss	3
MITCHEL	John		23	PETRIE	Margaret		22
MITCHEL	John		19	PETRIE	William		19
MITCHEL	Robert		5	PHILIP	Alexander		8
MITCHEL	Robert		26	PHILIP	John		11
MITCHEL	William		27	PIRIE		Mrs	8
MITCHEL	William		28	PIRIE	James		30
MITCHEL	William		20	PIRIE	John		20
MITCHEL	William		16	PIRIE	William		28
MITCHELL	William		30	PROTT	James		19

Surname	Chr.Names	Title	Page	Surname	Chr.Names	Title	Page
QUIRIE	Alexander		6	ROBERTSON	William		12
RAINIE	John		20	ROBERTSON	William		9
RAINIE	William		17	ROBERTSON	William		18
RAMSAY		Major	22	ROSS	David		20
RANTON	Thomas		8	ROSS	Donald		7
RAY	John		10	ROSS	James		15
REID		Mrs	15	ROSS	John		20
REID		Mr	20	SAMUEL	Andrew		25
REID		Mr	30	SAMUEL	Robert		30
REID		Mrs	8	SANDIE	James		27
REID	Alexander		27	SANGSTER		Widow	14
REID	Alexander		16	SANGSTER	George		23
REID	James		15	SANGSTER	James		7
REID	John		3	SANGSTER	James		23
REID	Peter		29	SANGSTER	John		11
RHIND	William		9	SANGSTER	Robert		13
RIACH	John		10	SANGSTER	William		26
RICHARD	James		27	SAUNDERS	John		4
RICHARD	John		27	SCANDRETT	James		18
RITCHIE	James		9	SCOTT		Mr	10
RITCHIE	Mary		9	SCOTT	Alexander		10
ROBB	Alexander		18	SCOTT	Alexander		20
ROBB	Andrew		17	SCOTT	James		23
ROBB	Andrew		14	SCOTT	John		28
ROBB	Elspet		12	SCOTT	John		23
ROBB	Elspet		9	SCOTT	Thomas		4
ROBB	Elspet		25	SCOTT	William		8
ROBB	George		14	SCOTT	William		2
ROBB	Jean		14	SCOTT	(junior)	Mr	6
ROBB	John		30	SELLER	John		10
ROBB	Mary		25	SELLER	John		24
ROBB	Peter		13	SELLER	Mary		24
ROBB	William		20	SELLER	William		9
ROBERTSON		Widow	23	SELLER	William		24
ROBERTSON		Mrs	5	SEMPLE	John		14
ROBERTSON		Mrs	3	SHAND		Mr	3
ROBERTSON		Baillie	17	SHARP		Mrs	16
ROBERTSON	Alexander		10	SHEWAN	Andrew		26
ROBERTSON	Alexander		14	SHEWAN	Robert		30
ROBERTSON	Alexander		13	SHEWAN	Robert		5
ROBERTSON	Andrew		2	SHIVES	Alexander		6
ROBERTSON	Christian		26	SHIVES	John		6
ROBERTSON	James		22	SHIVES	Robert		30
ROBERTSON	James		26	SHIVES	Robert		28
ROBERTSON	James		22	SHIVES	William		6
ROBERTSON	James		9	SIEVEWRIGHT	William		20
ROBERTSON	James		13	SIM		Mr	29
ROBERTSON	John		22	SIM	George		9
ROBERTSON	John		10	SIMPSON	Alexander		16
ROBERTSON	John		22	SIMPSON	Isabel		26
ROBERTSON	Joseph		19	SIMS		Mr	17
ROBERTSON	Thomas		9	SINCLAIR	Helen		9
ROBERTSON	Thomas		23	SKELTON	George		17
ROBERTSON	Thomas		2	SKELTON	James		16
ROBERTSON	Thomas		23	SKENE	Alexander		28
ROBERTSON	William		27	SKINNER	Margaret		11
ROBERTSON	William		8	SKINNER	Robert		18

Surname	Chr.Names	Title	Page	Surname	Chr.Names	Title	Page
SLAKER	James		12	STRATH	John		11
SLICER	Alexander		30	STUART	Charles		31
SLICER	George		20	STUART	James		14
SLICER	George		10	STUART	Thomas		17
SLORACH	John		15	SUMMERS	Robert		28
SMITH		Mrs	6	TAIT	Alexander		5
SMITH		Mr	19	TAIT	Jean		8
SMITH		Mrs	3	TAYLOR		Mrs	9
SMITH	Alexander		27	TAYLOR	Alexander		24
SMITH	Andrew		2	TAYLOR	Alexander		28
SMITH	Charles		12	TAYLOR	Andrew		28
SMITH	George		7	TAYLOR	Christian		13
SMITH	Isabel		21	TAYLOR	Isabel		18
SMITH	James		29	TAYLOR	James		24
SMITH	James		5	TAYLOR	Janet		24
SMITH	John		2	TAYLOR	Jean		24
SMITH	John		23	TAYLOR	John		7
SMITH	Thomas		4	TAYLOR	Margaret		19
SMITH	Thomas		7	TAYLOR	Marjory		25
SMITH	William		30	TAYLOR	Mary		23
SMITH	William		20	TAYLOR	William		18
SMITH	William		12	TAYLOR	William		14
SMITH	William		10	TAYLOR	William		14
SOUTTER		Mrs	12	THOM	Andrew		19
SOUTTER		Mrs	18	THOM	James		19
SOUTTER		Mrs	13	THOM	James		11
SOUTTER	Alexander		13	THOM	James		15
SOUTTER	Gilbert		13	THOM	John		21
SOUTTER	Janet		12	THOM	John		2
SOUTTER	Jean		24	THOM	John		11
SOUTTER	John		3	THOM	William		12
SOUTTER	John		8	THOMSON		Mrs	4
SOUTTER	Mary		14	THOMSON	Alexander		27
SOUTTER	William		14	THOMSON	Andrew		20
STEPHEN	Alexander		25	THOMSON	Elisabeth		18
STEPHEN	Christian		27	THOMSON	George		21
STEPHEN	George		25	THOMSON	James		8
STEPHEN	George		24	THOMSON	James		15
STEPHEN	John		24	THOMSON	William		14
STEPHEN	John		3	TODD		Mrs	9
STEPHEN	Margaret		25	TORRY		Mr	18
STEPHEN	Robert		25	TRAIL	James		10
STEPHEN	Robert		25	TRAIL	Jean		4
STEPHEN	Robert		24	TURRIFF	David		14
STEPHEN	William		25	TURRIFF	David		29
STEPHEN	William		24	URQUHART	John		29
STEPHEN	William		25	WALKER	James		19
STEPHEN	William		25	WALKER	John		26
STEPHEN	William		24	WALKER	William		26
STEVENSON	James		22	WALLACE	James		26
STEVENSON	William		12	WALLACE	Janet		14
STEWART		Mrs	7	WALLACE	John		17
STEWART	Patrick		17	WALLACE	John		30
STRACHAN	Alexander		13	WALLACE	William		15
STRACHAN	John		20	WARDEN	John		10
STRACHAN	John		30	WATSON	James		4
STRACHAN	William		8	WATSON	Janet		12

Surname	Chr.Names	Title	Page	Surname	Chr.Names	Title	Page
WATT	Christian		12	WILL	John		18
WATT	Thomas		11	WILL	William		10
WEBSTER		Widow	3	WILLIAMSON	James		4
WEBSTER	Elspet		19	WILLIAMSON	Robert		11
WEBSTER	James		12	WILLOX	George		9
WEBSTER	James		5	WILLOX	William		21
WEBSTER	James		5	WILSON		Mrs	3
WEBSTER	James		12	WILSON	Andrew		4
WEBSTER	John		15	WILSON	John		12
WEBSTER	John		25	WILSON	Theodore		4
WEBSTER	John		7	WOOD	Alexander		22
WEBSTER	William		28	WOOD	Alexander		19
WEMYSS	Walter		15	WOOD	George		16
WHITE	Alexander		7	WOOD	John		18
WHITECROSS	John		26	YEATS	Alexander		8
WHITECROSS	Margaret		26	YOUNGSON	John		16
WILL		Widow	29	YULE	Alexander		6
WILL	Alexander		15	YULE	James		21
WILL	Elisabeth		11	YULE	John		21